Unto Death

Freemasonry...
Freedom in Christ
or
Bondage to Lucifer?

Unto Death

Freemasonry...
Freedom in Christ
or
Bondage to Lucifer?

by: Barbara Cassada

Tome Publishing
Maryville, Tennessee

For additional copies of this book, please contact:

The Lion's Heart Ministries, Inc.

Email: bkcassada@gmail.com
http://www.thelionsheart.org

Library of Congress Cataloging-in-Publication Data
Cassada, Barbara, 1947-
Unto Death-Freemasonry...Freedom in Christ or Bondage to Lucifer /
Barbara Cassada
TZ4-791-233 1998

ISBN 1-928672-01-9

Published by Tome Publishing
909 Brown School Rd
Maryville TN 37804

Cover design by J. Tod Zeiger, II

TABLE OF CONTENTS

Chapter	Page
Introduction	7
1. Tracing the Roots	11
2. Soteriology of Freemasonry	17
3. Whom do they "really" worship?	21
4. Rites and Vows	27
5. Curses unto death	35
6. Freedom From Freemasonry	43
Endnotes	57
Appendix	59

INTRODUCTION

"...UNTO DEATH"

Romans 6:16

Know ye not, that to whom ye yield yourselves servants to obey, his servants ye are to whom ye obey;
whether of sin unto death, or of obedience unto righteousness?

1 Kings 18:21

Elijah went before the people and said,
"How long will you waver between two opinions?
If the LORD is God, follow him;
but if Baal is God, follow him."

Our friend George came to our church for the first time in June of 1994. It was a bit radical for his conservative, Evangelical upbringing; but on that first Sunday that he and his family came, God pulled out all the stops. We had a glorious and wonderfully charismatic service that day, and as for George, well, God got him! The following Sunday, he returned, again with his family, and this time brought his daughter, who was in her early twenties at that time. On this particular day, our speaker was an itinerant minister, who managed to get George's daughter baptized in the Holy Spirit, delivered a major prophecy over her life, and during the course of his message, completely offended George. That was because he had shared about a brother who had been delivered from Freemasonry. You see, George was a Mason. This was news to us, as we really hadn't thought about Masons very much. But we began to do a little surface research, and what we found was not good. As our concern began to grow, we felt God saying to us, "leave this one alone; I will take care of it." Sure enough, about three months after this incident, George called the local Lodge where he was a member, and told them that he was demitting. "I can't remain a member," George told them, "because you've taken Jesus Christ out of the Lodge." Not only was this significant in that it was completely accomplished supernaturally, but even more amazing was that George came from a family of Masons, and he was in line to succeed into a leadership position in his local lodge. Without anyone's help or assistance, God supernaturally turned George's heart, and delivered him of this foul curse.

One evening while discussing the Bible and healing, George made an offhand remark that seemed unrelated to the discussion. He offered that it seemed a large percentage of Masons were developing colon or prostate cancer. We did not pursue that avenue of discussion. The comment stayed with me, however, and two years later came bounding to the forefront of my thinking.

Traveling around the globe with Pastor/Evangelist Randy Clark from St. Louis, Missouri afforded my husband and I many opportunities to pray for persons in need of physical or emotional healing. In many cases, as we asked the Holy Spirit for discernment to know in which direction to pray, we uncovered the fact that Freemasonry existed in the family of those being prayed for. As my curiosity intensified, I began to ask people with certain specific infirmities if they or their family were involved in Freemasonry. I was astonished to discover that almost everyone answered in the affirmative. Primarily continuous miscarriages, colon cancers, prostate cancers, breast cancer, heart problems, organ malfunctions, Crone's disease, brain tumors, Parkinson's, Alzheimer's, and pre-mature death of children or relatives were among the primary concerns for which we discovered Freemasonry ties.

Knowing little to nothing about the Freemasons, my husband and I began a quest for knowledge about this most universally influential organization. What we discovered was diabolical and frightening in the intensity of its deception. Many situations we prayed for could be directly traced to the vows (curses) that Masons pronounce over themselves in each degree of elevation within this secret society. As a Freemason traverses the ladder of degrees from the very first oath as an Entered Apprentice, he binds himself ever more tightly to the diabolical schemes of the enemy. The Satanic rites are performed under the guise of following God, but when the light of truth is shined upon them, the reality of doctrine becomes crystal clear. The Word promises us that Satan will come as "an angel of light". In doing good for the community, the Freemasons and all attendant secret organizations following in its path (Mormonism, Elks, Shriners, Foresters, Moose, etc.) weave a web of deception that succors the heart of man into a loving fellowship and needed camaraderie, then binds that heart to itself with fear for the consequences of betrayal.

Even though we can trace the connection of some of our founding fathers to Masonry, we do not find reference to those connections in history books. Masons have always been adept at keeping hidden what they did not want known. That is, however, until recently when more and more Christian men have left the Lodge under conviction of the Holy Spirit and have broken their "sacred" vows revealing the dogma behind the mystique. I am grateful that the light is being shown on this organization that appears as "an angel of light". I can add very little to what has already been written, but as I see more and more God-fearing, Christian brothers and sisters become affected with the life-taking diseases wrought by the enemy to destroy the Body of Christ, I feel a need to add my comments to those already published.

Just as different communities and lodges developed based on preference and location, so we see now on the earth different lodges professing different yet strikingly similar creeds. This booklet is not meant to bring an in-depth study of the origins of the York Rite, Scottish Rite, etc. It is meant simply to help the average person bound by Masonic curses gain a general understanding of Freemasonry roots in order that they may attain freedom from a vantage point of knowledge. A list of excellent sources is found in the last chapter and this author refers anyone to those sources who has a keener interest to study further.

CHAPTER 1

TRACING THE ROOTS

Isaiah 14:12-14

"How you are fallen from heaven,
O Lucifer, son of the morning!
How you are cut down to the ground,
You who weakened the nations!
For you have said in your heart:
'I will ascend into heaven,
I will exalt my throne above the stars of God;
I will also sit on the mount of the congregation
On the farthest sides of the north;
I will ascend above the heights of the clouds,
I will be like the Most High.'

Since the original fall of Lucifer from heaven there has been one purpose in his warped thinking—that of having a throne, exalting it above the stars and being like the Most High. His deceptions have been subtle and crafty throughout the ages, but none seems to be more extensive, long-lived, or diabolically carried out as the one we are examining.

Masons themselves cannot agree on the origin of their organization as it has always been enshrined in secrecy. When the writings of renowned men, leaders in Freemasonry, are studied, however, connections to Egypt, Baal worship, the Tower of Babel, Solomon's temple, and other Biblical events become evident. The earliest Biblical reference found in the *Encyclopedia of Freemasonry* refers us to Noah, the patriarch of the human race following the flood. It discusses Noah and his three sons departing Mount Ararat, dwelling in Shinar where they "commenced the building of a lofty tower." [1] A lofty tower was indeed built by Nimrod, the great grandson of Noah.

> He was a mighty hunter before the LORD; that is why it is said, "Like Nimrod, a mighty hunter before the LORD." The first centers of his kingdom were **Babylon**, Erech, Akkad and Calneh, in Shinar." (Genesis. 10:9-10)
>
> Now the whole world had one language and a common speech. As men moved eastward, they found a plain in Shinar and settled there. They said to each other, "Come, let's make bricks and bake them thoroughly." They used **brick instead of stone**, and tar for mortar. Then they said, "Come, let us build ourselves a city, with a tower that reaches to the heavens, so that we may make a name for ourselves and not be scattered over the face of the whole earth."
> But the LORD came down to see the city and the tower that the men were building. The LORD said, "If as one people speaking the same language they have begun to do this, then nothing they plan to do will be impossible for them. Come, let us go down and confuse their language so they will not understand each other."
>
> So the LORD scattered them from there

> over all the earth, and they stopped building the city. That is why it was called Babel—because there the LORD confused the language of the whole world. From there the LORD scattered them over the face of the whole earth. (Genesis 11:1-10)

In the Tower of Babel we see the same spirit working his plan for glory as in Isaiah 14:12-14. Lucifer was still seeking a throne from where he could receive worship and reign supreme over all the earth. Historical accounts reveal that Nimrod became a god to his people. After the destruction of Babel and the confusion of languages, his name took on many forms. According to *The Bible Knowledge Commentary*:

> Written Babylonian accounts of the building of the city of Babylon refer to its construction in heaven by the gods as a celestial city, as an expression of pride (*Enuma Elish* VI, lines 55-64). These accounts say it was made by the same process of brick making described in verse 3, with every brick inscribed with the name of the Babylonian god Marduk.
>
> Also the ziggurat, the step-like tower believed to have been first erected in Babylon, was said to have its top in the heavens (cf. v. 4). This artificial mountain became the center of worship in the city, a miniature temple being at the top of the tower. The Babylonians took great pride in their building; they boasted of their city as not only impregnable, but also as the heavenly city, baub-ili ("the gate of God").

> The account in Genesis views this city as the predominant force in the world; the epitome of ungodly powers, in a word, the "anti-kingdom.[2]

One of the names inscribed on the bricks was that of Baal. From here we connect to the Egyptian pagan religions. Albert Pike[3] in his *Morals and Dogma* makes the connection for us when he discusses the feast of initiations commemorating the Creation and honoring "Thor, the Prince of the Power of the Air".[4] He describes the celebration, which includes Thor as the Sun, the Egyptian gods Osiris and Kneph, and the Phoenician god Bel or Baal. This connection is critical to our understanding of the demonic powers underlying Freemasonry. The legend of Osiris is interwoven into the ritual of the Third Degree or Master Mason.

Osiris, the primary god of Egypt was allegedly killed by his brother, his body nailed in a coffin, and thrown into the Nile. His sister and wife, Isis, retrieved his body but lost it again to the jealous brother who, hoping to destroy it forever, cut it up into fourteen pieces and scattered it throughout the kingdom. Isis once again retrieves all the parts except for the phallus, which was supposedly eaten by a crab. She then crafts a phallus for the body and embalms the once again whole body. Embalming becomes the method of preserving the body in order for the immortal soul to be carried into the afterlife. Osiris from this time forward is known as the Lord of the Underworld, the god of the sun, and the god of fertility. He is one of three gods whose names are linked together in the secret name of god as revealed in the Royal Arch Mason degree (to be covered later). Further, the phallus, represented by the obelisk in Masonry, is one of the main symbols used in that cult. You will find a masonically edicated obelisk in most major capitols of the world and as the grave markers of high Masons that have passed on. The Osirian cycle of death, burial, recovery, reburial, and immortality is then carried into a Biblical connection that draws in the uninformed Christian.

This final spiritual connection is in Solomon's Temple. Some Masons claim their Masonic roots come from the building of this temple known as God's dwelling place. However, no evidence has been unearthed to validate this assertion. It would seem the Solomon connection was later added to appeal to Christians. The legend of Huram, King of Tyre, master builder for portions of the temple is dramatically perverted and rings similar to the legend of Osiris. According to legend Hiram was asked by scoundrels for a secret word from the Master. When he refused, he was killed by a blow to the head with a mallet. After burial, retrieval, and reburial, Hiram is raised from the dead by the strength of his master's, Solomon's, hand. . This particular legend of Huram's (Hiram) death, burial, and resurrection is played out with each candidate for the Third Degree or Master Mason.

We have a spiritual connection, now we will look at the natural connection. The builders chose to use bricks on which they could inscribe the names of their gods rather than stones, which would be harder to transport and set in place. The craftsman builders are the first reference to Masons. We have many Biblical references to brick making especially at the time of Israel's bondage in Egypt. This craft continued to develop as the builders, stonecutters, brick makers, and inscribers of stone erected temples and monuments throughout the known world. The cutting and inscribing of stone was done primarily in workshops where the brick could remain dry and be worked more effectively. By the 13th century A.D., these workshops were referred to as lodges and began to take on social application as well as places of employment. Different lodges had different passwords and hand signals that identified its members to each other due mainly to the high percentage of illiteracy. As the architecture changed and evolved, the Mason's found they had less and less work; but to continue the other social aspects of their lodges non-tradesmen were invited to join. These were referred to as "Speculative Masons".

These Speculative Masons, generally leaders in their respective communities, eventually took control of the lodges. As governments and the church became more controlling and corrupt the lodges began to go underground. They established a freedom of religious worship and an underlying program to set up a New World order. Just as Lucifer attempted to install a one-world government in Babylon from which he would reign supreme, so he continues his attempts to this very day. He will eventually accomplish this during the Tribulation period as outlined in the Book of Revelation, but it will be short-lived. This plan has been subtly woven through the fabric of world history following one conqueror after another such as Napoleon, Hitler, and others with the final despot being revealed as Antichrist.

CHAPTER 2

SOTERIOLOGY OF FREEMASONRY

Ephesians 2:8

For it is by grace you have
been saved, through faith—
and this not from yourselves,
it is the gift of God—

Acts 4:12

Salvation is found in no one else,
for there is no other name under heaven
given to men by which we must be saved.

Although most Masons deny that Freemasonry is a religion, Albert Pike in his book *Morals and Dogma* stated emphatically, "Every masonic lodge is a temple of religion, and its teachings are instructions in religion."[5] The religious doctrine of Freemasonry is based on salvation by works as evidenced from the very first rite performed for the initiate Mason. As the newly accepted member is brought in as an Entered Apprentice, he is presented with a "Lamb Skin" or "White Leather Apron." This apron embodies the cultic symbolism of Mason's erroneous deception. It is considered to be the emblem of innocence "more ancient than the Golden Fleece; more honorable than the Star and Garter, or any other order that can be conferred upon you at this or any future period by King, Prince or Potentate, or any other person, except he be a Mason and in the body of a Lodge".[6]

This apron is to remind the Mason that his life is to be pure, full of noble deeds, and always striving for greater achievements. It sounds good, but it does not buy salvation as the Lodge professes. George Thornburgh expresses the Mason's faith in the protection afforded by the lambskin apron in the following quote:

> The lamb has in all ages been deemed an emblem of innocence. The lambskin is therefore to remind you of that purity of life and conduct which is so *essentially necessary to your gaining admission* to the Celestial Lodge above, where the Supreme Architect of the Universe presides. (Italics added)[7]

He further underscores the function of the apron by stating its final purpose:

> And when at last your weary feet shall have come to the end of life's toilsome journey, and from your nerveless grasp shall drop forever the working tools of life, may the *record of your life* and actions be as pure and spotless as this fair emblem which I place in your hands. And when your trembling soul shall stand naked and alone before the *Great White Throne*, there to receive judgment for the deeds done while here in the body, may it be your portion to hear from Him who sitteth as the Judge Supreme the welcome words: "Well, done, thou good and faithful servant; thou has been faithful over a few things, I will make

> thee ruler over many things; enter thou into the joy of the Lord." (Italics added)[8]

From this first degree upward the Mason is drawn more fully into the deception. The Great White Throne judgment spoken of in Revelation, Chapter 20, is set aside specifically for the dead judged for their works. These are not the "dead in Christ", but those that refused His salvation and strove to enter heaven on their good works. No works performed on this earth can stand up to the ultimate work of redemption by Jesus Christ with His death on the cross and resurrection. For a Mason to even consider that he will stand at the Great White Throne is an admission that he does not accept Christ as his savior.

The prayers contained in the first three degrees sound Christian and are spoken from the Bible. They are, however, only used as further entrapment of the already deceived individual who would take the vows of obedience to the Masonic Lodge and its precepts.

Jesus Christ commanded his followers to go into all the world and preach the gospel. His gospel is the only source of truth for He alone came to save the world. Mark 16:15 reads, "He said to them, 'Go into all the world and preach the good news to all creation'". Masonry, however, forbids evangelism in any form. The god of Freemasonry is in direct conflict with the God of the Bible for its god is generic in order that no religious affiliation need be offended.

> To respect all forms of worship, to tolerate all political and religious opinions; not to blame, and still less to condemn the religion of others; *not to seek to make converts*;

> but to be content if they have the religion of Socrates; a veneration for the Creator, the religion of good works, and grateful acknowledgement of God's blessings. (Italics added)[9]

Further evidence that Masons do not look to Jesus Christ as savior is found in the fact that Freemasonry supports all religions. Upon the altar rests the Christian's Bible as well as other books of religious organizations and is considered to be only one among equals. One may find the Muslim Koran, the Book of Mormon, the Hindu Vedas, books from the Christian Scientist, Spiritist, Unitarian, Buddhist, Baha'i, Taoist, Jehovah's Witness, and any others who wish to express their devotion to the Lodge.

In study of Masonic inclusion, all races and cultures are welcome. Since some of these cultures such as the Jews, Turks, or Chinese reject either the New or Old Testament, belief in the Bible is not required, as it would preclude the membership of all but Christians. Masonry is not founded on the Bible or Christian teachings as some profess it to be. It is, in fact, founded on mystic cults that profess belief in any god to the exclusion of the One True God.

CHAPTER 3

WHOM DO THEY "REALLY" WORSHIP?

Luke 4:8
Jesus answered, "It is written
'Worship the Lord your God and serve him only.'"

John 14:6

Jesus answered, "I am the way
and the truth and the life.
No one comes to the Father except through me".

Exodus 23:13

Be careful to do everything I have said to you.
Do not invoke the names of other gods;
do not let them be heard on your lips.

Since his encounter with Eve in the Garden of Eden, Satan has continually brought a lie wrapped in truth to see if we will take his deceptive package. The deception woven into the fabric of Freemasonry is not just an attempt to lead the initiate down a secret path to Lucifer worship, but each ritual displays a blatant mockery of the redemptive work of Jesus Christ. His name, no longer spoken within the walls of a lodge, has even been removed from Scripture used in ceremony. Jesus Christ, the only gate to heaven is denied His place in history and, more importantly, His place at the right hand of the Father.

The Masonic deception is even announced in Pike's *Morals and Dogma*, which makes loyalty to Freemasonry's rites and secrets even more ludicrous. He specifically refers to the first three degrees more commonly known as the Blue Lodge in the following statement:

> The Blue Degrees are but the outer court or portico of the Temple. Part of the symbols are displayed there to the Initiate, but he is intentionally misled by false interpretations. It is not intended that he shall understand them; but it is intended that he shall imagine he understands them.[10]

One of the key symbols displayed on every Masonic lodge shows the compass and level with a capital "G" in the center. The Initiate is told that the "G" stands for the "Great Architect of the Universe" who is his god. He begins his quest for the secret word, supposedly the real name of God lost during the building of Solomon's Temple. Not until he attains the 7th degree or Royal Arch does he find the secret name of the deity that rules over Freemasonry. He is told the name with a reverence and awe that should be reserved for God alone. This name, "JAHBULON", is triune in blasphemous mockery of the true triune God of the universe. "JAH" is the shortened form of the Hebrew name "YAHWEH" or "JEHOVAH" which Christians know to be one of the names of God. "BUL" is another rendering of "BAAL", the pagan god of the Bible. "ON" was the word used to call upon the

Babylonian deity "OSIRIS." This name is so sacred among the Masons that no Royal Arch Mason can pronounce the name alone. It takes three Masons to pronounce this "sacred" name. This name is used in further rites and vows made by Masons in their climb up the Masonic pyramid.

If this blasphemy were not enough, once the 30th, 31st, and 32nd degrees are attained, the real god of Freemasonry is revealed, no longer hidden behind innuendoes. Albert Pike was quoted as saying:

> That which we must say to a crowd is – We worship a God, but it is the God that one adores without superstition. To you, Sovereign Grand Inspectors General, we say this, that you may repeat it to the Brethren of the 32nd, 31st, and 30th degrees – The Masonic religion should be, by all of us initiates of the high degrees, maintained in the purity of the Luciferian Doctrine. If Lucifer were not God, would Adonay whose deeds prove his cruelty, perdify and hatred of man, barbarism and repulsion for science, would Adonay and his priests, calumniate him? Yes, Lucifer is God, and unfortunately Adonay is also god. For the eternal law is that there is no light without shade no beauty without ugliness, no white without black, for the absolute can only exist as two gods: darkness being necessary to the statue, and the brake to the locomotive. Thus, the doctrine of Satanism is a heresy; and the true and pure philosophical religion is the belief in Lucifer, the equal of Adonay; but Lucifer, God of

> Light and God of Good, is struggling for humanity against Adonay, the God of Darkness and Evil."[11]

Within Pike's comments a true statement does occur. Lucifer is indeed struggling for humanity against Adonay for he is ever seeking the worship that is due Adonay alone. Further he is seeking the destruction of man, who alone can worship the Father in spirit and in truth.

> 1 Peter 5:8
>
> Be self-controlled and alert. Your enemy the devil prowls around like a roaring lion looking for someone to devour.

Few Masons today seem to know the name of Albert Pike and if they do, they deny his influence over Freemasonry. However, Pike's authority within the Lodge stands and his profession of its dogma is not dispelled simply because man chooses to deny his influence. It would be like saying Satan does not exist simply because I will it to be so. What foolishness! One final quote seals the worship for Freemasonry solidly in Luciferian doctrine—

> Lucifer, the Light-bearer! Strange and mysterious name to give to the Spirit of Darkness! Lucifer, the son of the morning! Is it he who bears the Light, and with it's splendors intolerable blinds feeble, sensual or selfish Souls? Doubt it not![12]

Such blasphemy is at the heart of Freemasonry. How any Christian brother could be wrapped so tightly in this deception is a mystery. The choice is crystal clear. There is only one light-bearer, one whose splendor lights the heavens, one bright Morning Star, one who lights every man that comes into the world—the only Jesus Christ, Son of the most High God.

> John 8:12 When Jesus spoke again to the people, he said, "I am the light of the world. Whoever follows me will never walk in darkness, but will have the light of life."
>
> Revelation 22:16 "I, Jesus, have sent my angel to give you this testimony for the churches. I am the Root and the Offspring of David, and the bright Morning Star."

CHAPTER 4

RITES AND VOWS

Matthew 5:34-37
But I tell you, Do not swear at all: either by heaven, for it is God's throne; or by the earth, for it is his footstool;
or by Jerusalem, for it is the city of the Great King.
And do not swear by your head,
for you cannot make even one hair white or black.
Simply let your 'Yes' be 'Yes,' and your 'No,' 'No';
anything beyond this comes from the evil one.

James 5:12

Above all, my brothers, do not swear—
not by heaven or by earth or by anything else.
Let your "Yes" be yes, and your "No," no,
or you will be condemned.

Every Mason from the 1st degree on up maintains his brotherhood in the Lodge by vows of secrecy and allegiance. He swears in the name of God to abide by the oaths, which he takes at each step up the pyramid. To swear by God is a sacrilege in itself; but to do so in a pagan ritual that mocks the work of Christ is to bring oneself under sentence of death. Each progressive oath becomes more obscene and bloody in its implications. Listed below are several of the penalty oaths sworn to each Mason initiated into the Lodge and at each degree as represented. The Bible clearly states that life and death are in the power of the tongue. Not only are Christians required to avoid oaths, they are commanded to speak only those things which are edifying and minister grace. If we speak blood oaths over ourselves, are we not binding our lives to the power of those oaths? I believe we are. In fact, as head of the household and spiritual authority therein, the man not only binds himself, he binds his family and future generations to the consequences embodied in that oath. There are many examples in the Bible of God's commands regarding foolish oaths and of generations suffering as a result of their forefathers covenant words spoken contrary to God.

We will now look at the blood oaths spoken by the Masons which reek of Satanic covenant and blatantly violate the Word of God.

1st Degree – Entered Apprentice

To all of which I most solemnly and sincerely promise and swear with a firm and steadfast resolution to keep and perform the same without the least equivocation, mental reservation or self evasion, whatsoever: binding myself under a no less penalty than that of having my throat cut from ear to ear, my tongue torn out by the roots and buried in the rough sands of the sea at low water mark where the tide ebbs and flows twice in twenty-four hours, should I in the least knowingly or willfully violate or transgress this my entered apprentice obligation. So help me God and keep me steadfast.

2nd Degree – Fellow Craft

To all of which I most solemnly and sincerely promise and swear with a steadfast resolution to keep and perform the same without the least equivocation, mental reservation, or self evasion whatsoever, binding myself under a no less penalty than that of having my left breast torn open, my heart plucked from thence and given to the wild beasts of the field and the fowls of the air as a prey; should I in the least knowingly or willfully violate this, my fellow craft obligation. So help me God and keep me steadfast.

3rd Degree – Master Mason

To all of which I most solemnly and sincerely promise and swear with a firm and steadfast resolution to keep and perform the same without the least equivocation, mental reservation or self evasion whatsoever, binding myself under no less a penalty, than that of having my body severed in twain, my bowels taken from thence and burned to ashes and they scattered to the four winds of heaven that there might remain no remembrance among men or Masons, of so vile a wretch as I would be, should I in the least knowingly or willfully violate or transgress this my Master mason obligation. So help me God and keep me steadfast.

In this 3rd Degree the Osiris/Hiram connection raises its ugly head in a blasphemous ritual that mocks the work of Christ. The initiate is laid on the floor as if dead. After two attempts by lesser Degree Masons, the Worshipful Master (representing King Solomon) successfully raises the candidate with the "Strong Grip" or "Lion's Paw Grip" and he is thus "reborn." The Master Mason further swears:

> I will not give the grand hailing sign of distress, except I am in real distress...and should I ever see that sign given, or the word accompanying it, and the person who gave it appearing to be in distress, I will fly to his relief, at the risk of my life, should there be a greater probability of saving his life than of losing my own...I will not speak evil of a brother mason neither behind his back, nor before his face, but will apprise him of all approaching danger, if in my power...a master mason's secrets given to me in charge as such, and I knowing him to be such, shall remain as secure and inviolable in my breast as in his own, before communicated to me, murder and treason excepted, and they left at my own election.

The words "murder and treason excepted" were not part of the original oath, but were added later. These become the only two crimes for which the Mason may, by conscience, refuse aid to a fellow Mason. The famous case of William Morgan, a Royal Arch Mason abducted and murdered by fellow Masons in 1826, is the most heinous example of the loyalty given by Masons one to another as well as an extreme example of the brutal enforcement of oaths made within the Lodge. Mr. Morgan chose for some inexplicable reason to publish the secrets of the Lodge and was killed for his violation of Masonic trust. In a document entitled *The Proceedings of the United States Anti-Masonic Convention* we find these words:

> Morgan's blood was shed, without any pretence that he had infringed the laws of the land, and with little or no private malice, on the part of those by whom he fell. The persons most deeply implicated, in the guilt of his fall, were industrious, intelligent, and reputable citizens, bound to life and to society, by all the usual ties. They did not proceed hastily, nor adopt their ultimate decision, without manifest and painful reluctance. Before they took his life, they deliberated, earnestly, frequently, and long, upon their masonic obligations. These obligations they thought binding. He had certainly and essentially violated them. The unanimous result of all their deliberations was, that he must die. And in the understanding of all masonic exposition, as well as of common sense, if the obligations were binding, they were right, in their decision.[13]

This oath for the Royal Arch Mason is extremely frightening when you consider that so many leaders are involved in this organization and they are sworn to protect each other's secrets. This applies even if those secrets involve violations of the law. Should a judge sitting on the bench receive the Masonic sign from a defendant, he finds himself more bound to his brother in the lodge than to the law which he has sworn to uphold. The same is true for law enforcement officers, lawyers, solicitors, barristers, etc. regardless of nationality. Wherever Freemasonry exists, loyalty to a fellow mason takes precedent over right and wrong. Can we truly accept as Christian an organization whose members would honor the code of that establishment over those of God and their country? Surely this is an abhorrent abomination in the sight of an almighty, righteous God. His command is clear as stated in Leviticus 5:1, "'If a person sins because he does not speak up when he hears a public charge to testify regarding something he has seen or learned about, he will be held responsible."

7th Degree – Royal Arch Mason (from the York Rite)

I furthermore promise and swear, that I will assist a Companion Royal Arch Mason when I see him engaged in any difficulty and will espouse his cause so far as to extricate him from the same, where he be right or wrong...To all which I do most solemnly and sincerely promise and swear, with a firm and steadfast resolution to keep and perform the same, without any equivocation, mental reservation, or self evasion of mind in me whatever; binding myself under no less penalty, than to have my skull smote off, and my brains exposed to the scorching rays of the Meridian sun, should I knowingly or willfully violate or transgress any part of this my solemn oath or obligation of a Royal Arch Mason. So help me God, and keep me steadfast.

The vile oaths become more and more horrendous as one swears curses upon his own body and soul. The 18th Degree of the Scottish Rite once again mocks the work of Jesus Christ as the candidate accepts the penalty of forever being deprived of the true word (and this is the missing word or name of God, not the word as Christians know it) and to be kept in perpetual darkness. He also accepts that violation of his vows will cause his blood to run continually from his body and gall mixed with vinegar will be his constant drink (reminiscent of Jesus on the cross). Further mockery of Jesus is spoken from the Mason's mouth when he accepts the penalty of sharp thorns being his pillow and death on the cross his completed punishment. All this is sworn in the name of God and sealed with a kiss on the Bible.

In the 10th Degree of the Scottish Rite the Mason accepts a bloody consequence of disobedience and further swears to be ready to inflict the same punishment on a fellow Mason should he break any obligation to the Lodge and his oath. The 30th Degree of the Scottish Rite requires an oath under penalty of death should the candidate not only reveal what he knows, but disobey any statute of his Lodge.

Finally, when the candidate attains the 32nd Degree he becomes eligible to join the ranks of the Shriners. During civic activities where Shriners march, we have all seen the little red hat they wear. I always thought it was rather funny. The truth of the matter is, its roots are ominous and anything but funny. Ed Decker writes:

> Worn and even carried to the grave with pompous dignity, the history of the Fez is barbaric and anti-Christian. In the early 8th century, Muslim hordes overran the Moroccan city of Fez, shouting, "*There is no god but Allah and Mohammed is his prophet.*" There, they butchered approximately 50,000 Christians. These men, women and children were slain because of their faith in Christ, all in the

> name of Allah, the same demon god to whom every Shriner must bow, with hands tied behind his back, in worship, proclaiming him the god of his fathers in the Shrine initiation, at the Altar of Obligation... During the butchering of the people of Fez, the streets literally ran red with the blood of the martyred Christians. The muslim murderers dipped their caps in the blood of their victims as a testimony to Allah. These blood stained caps eventually were called *Fezzes* and became a badge of honor for those who killed a Christian. The Shriners wear that same red Fez today. The greatest tragedy is that the Fez is often worn by men who profess to be Christians themselves. It must cause God to weep.[14]

For a Christian to become so deeply involved in Freemasonry and not even question the roots of the organization or the source of its symbols and vows underscores the magnitude of its deception. Every rite performed and every oath sworn by a Mason takes him deeper into demonic bondage. Proverbs 18:21 tell us, "The tongue has the power of life and death, and those who love it will eat its fruit." The vows by Mason's produce fruit in their lives and the lives of succeeding generations. We need not call them vows or oaths, but we should call them what they really are, "curses."

CHAPTER 5

CURSES UNTO DEATH

Deuteronomy 30:19

This day I call heaven and earth
as witnesses against you
that I have set before you life and death,
blessings and curses.
Now choose life, so that you and your children may live

Exodus 20:5

You shall not bow down to them or worship them;
for I, the LORD your God, am a jealous God,
punishing the children for the sin of the fathers
to the third and fourth generation
of those who hate me,

Proverbs 18:20-21

From the fruit of his mouth a man's stomach is filled;
with the harvest from his lips he is satisfied.
The tongue has the power of life and death,
and those who love it will eat its fruit.

The Bible is very clear about the power in our words. Words are the fruit of our mouth, either good or bad, and that fruit grows generation after generation unless the source is uprooted. It is quite obvious that the oaths sworn in Freemasonry are not blessings but curses. When a man kneels at an altar and swears an oath to God, he is making a willful decision to choose either life or death, blessings or curses. God commands us in Deuteronomy 30:19 to choose life. Why? So that we and *our children* may live. It is clear from this passage of scripture and the following that our choices affect the lives of subsequent generations.

> Hebrews 7:9-10 One might even say that Levi, who collects the tenth, paid the tenth through Abraham, because when Melchizedek met Abraham, Levi was still in the body of his ancestor.

Levi, a descendant of Abraham, is said to have paid the tithe since he was in Abraham's loins. A mystery, perhaps, but one that is clearly a Biblical principal set down in God's Word for us to understand. The choices we make affect our children and our children's children.

We know the sins of our fathers can be visited upon us as even the Apostles understood this fact when they were walking with Jesus. In John 9:2, "His disciples asked him, "'Rabbi, who sinned, this man or his parents, that he was born blind?'" Why else would they ask such a question unless it was understood that this was a real possibility?

During our travels, praying for people, and studying about curses, we have found many instances where people could not get free of bondage or healed of physical ailments until generational curses had been broken in their lives. There are many books written about generational curses and how they apply to Christian so I will not discuss the subject in depth here. Suffice it to say that as we prayed and the Holy Spirit revealed the source of the curse, the person was able to break its hold over their lives and freedom came. In the cases of physical ailments, I became frustrated when our prayers seemed fruitless. We would pray in the area of deliverance and many times see results. Many times, however, it would seem that we encountered brick walls and no breakthrough was sensed. The Holy Spirit began leading me to ask these seemingly difficult cases if anyone in their family line had been involved in Freemasonry. Almost to a person, the answer was "yes." Sending out an inquiry as to Masonic connections and family history of illness produced many responses, some of which are listed below. We have since found many ministries involved in breaking Masonic curses and the results they have witnessed. Around the world this issue is being addressed with healings and deliverances increasing as these diabolical ties are broken. Here are just a few of the family histories we have received of persons with family involvement in Freemasonry:

Kristi: **Connection** —Step-father Mason
Conditions — Manic-depressive, Satanic ritual abuse, Multiple Personality Disorder

George: **Connection** — Father Mason
Conditions — heart by-pass surgery, manic-depressive; Father died of heart problems

Allen: **Connection** – DeMolay; Paternal Great Grandfather and Grandmother, Paternal Uncle, Masons
Conditions — Multiple Personality Disorder, Post Traumatic Stress Disorder, suicide tendencies, migraine headaches, bleeding ulcers,

homosexuality, clinical depression; Mother – breast cancer, mental instability, migraine headaches, heart disease; Sister – miscarriages, breast cancer (same area as mother), divorce; Father – Parkinson's, prostate cancer, committed suicide; Paternal aunt – Multi-infarct dementia; Paternal uncle – Water on the brain, died violent and insane; Paternal grandfather – cancer of the mouth; Paternal great uncle – cancer of the throat; Paternal grandmother – heart disease; Paternal great-grandmother – breast cancer

Karen: **Connection** — Family member, Mason; self, Triangle Girls

Condition — lupus

Don: **Connection** — Masons in both Father's and Mother's family lines

Conditions — Infertility; Sister – Marfan's syndrome resulting in open-heart surgery, pancreatic cancer

Kathleen: **Connection** — Father, Shriner; Brother, ex-Mason; husband's grandfather, Mason

Conditions — Father – glaucoma, gall bladder difficulty; Son – autism, allergies; Husband's family – cancer through the generations

Polly: **Connection** — Father, Mason; Maternal Grandfather, Shriner

Conditions — Grandfather – heart problems; Grandmother – congestive heart failure; Father – massive heart failure; Husband's maternal grandfather – stroke victim; Husband's maternal grandmother – Alzheimer's; Siblings – allergies;

Daughter – allergies

Marty: **Connection** — Paternal Grandfather, Mason

Conditions Chronic digestive problems, dizziness, head pain; Father – pancreatic disease; Brother – pancreatic disease

David: **Connection** — Father-in-law, Mason

Conditions — Wife's father — depression; wife – bowel problems; mother-in-law – memory trouble

Kirk: **Connection** — Paternal Grandmother, Eastern Star; Paternal Grandfather, Mason-32nd Degree

Conditions — Paternal grandmother – Alzheimer's, glaucoma, cataracts, phlebitis, high blood pressure; Paternal grandfather – emphysema; Uncle – allergies; Father – intestinal polyps, hemorrhoids, prostate problems, sinus problems

Martin: **Connection** — Self, Mason, Wife's Grandfather, Mason

Conditions — brain tumors, menengiomas, prostate removal; financial losses

Barbara: **Connection** — Father, Mason

Conditions — death of a premature baby; three miscarriages, gall bladder removed; Father – gall bladder removal; Mother – gall stones, hysterectomy, heart attack, senility, hiatus hernia, defective kidneys; Sister– irritable bowel syndrome

Lucy: **Connection** — Great Grandfather, Mason-33rd Degree; Grandfather, Mason-33rd Degree

Conditions — Paternal Grandfather – Alzheimer's, heart failure; Uncle – homosexual; Aunt – heart problems, ulcers, arthritis, depression; Father – alcoholism, manic depression, heart problems, cancer of the lungs; Sister – Crone's, kidney disease; Maternal Grandfather – heart attack, alcoholism; Aunt – several miscarriages, two children premature death; Mother, heart problems

Frank: **Connection** — Grandfather, Mason; Father, Mason

Conditions — Sister – hysterectomy; Second sister – four miscarriages; Father – hardening of arteries, lack of oxygen to brain

Mandri: **Connection** — Father, Mason
Condition — Several miscarriages

Irene: **Connection** — Grandfather, Mason
Condition — Crone's disease

Corina: **Connection** — Grandfather, Mason
Condition — Brain tumor.

Barbara: **Connection** — Father, Mason; Mother, Eastern Star

Conditions — Father, heart attack; Mother, Multiple Sclerosis, arthritis; self, lack of finances.

These are obviously only a sampling of the information we have acquired in our quest for understanding. Obviously those conditions listed above do not occur exclusively due to Masonic connections. However, there is enough evidence in the Bible regarding generational curses to know that a connection does exist. Also, various ministries have seen dramatic results when praying off these curses. Sin and curses do indeed travel down blood lines. We must not be ignorant of the enemy's devises.

When praying for the sick and seeing no breakthrough and when other deliverance prayer seems to be hitting a brick wall, we look for Masonic connections for the following infirmities (the list can and will include others illnesses associated with the curses spoken against various areas of the body):

Allergies
Alzheimers
Anger
Anorexia
Asthma
Brain tumors
Breast cancer
Colon cancer
Crone's
Dyslexia
Fears
Heart problems
Infant death
Infertility
Insanity
Lupus
Intestinal Diseases
Miscarriage
Molestation
Parkinsons
Pre-mature death
Secretiveness
Prostate cancer

CHAPTER 6

FREEDOM FROM FREEMASONRY

Leviticus 5:4-5

Or if a person thoughtlessly takes an oath to do anything, whether good or evil—in any matter one might carelessly swear about—even though he is unaware of it, in any case when he learns of it he will be guilty. When anyone is guilty in any of these ways, he must confess in what way he has sinned.

1 John 2:1

My dear children, I write this to you so that you will not sin. But if anybody does sin, we have one who speaks to the Father in our defense— Jesus Christ, the Righteous One.

1 John 1:9

If we confess our sins, he is faithful and just and will forgive us our sins and purify us from all unrighteousness.

The good news is that we have an advocate who sits at the right hand of God. We can confess "in what way" we have sinned, be forgiven, and be purified from the unrighteousness of the curse. By renouncing the curse we cancel the authority of Satan to bring the effects of those curses into our lives. The following is copied verbatim from Selwyn Stevens, *Unmasking Freemasonry-Removing the Hoodwink*, with permission:

If you or someone you love is a descendant of a Mason, I recommend that you pray through the following prayer from your heart. Don't be like the Masons – please read it through first so you know what is involved. It is best to pray this aloud with a Christian witness or counselor present.

"Father God, creator of heaven and earth, I come to you in the name of Jesus Christ your Son. I come as a sinner seeking forgiveness and cleansing from all sins committed against you, and others made in your image. I honor my earthly father and mother and all of my ancestors of flesh and blood, and of the spirit by adoption and godparents, but I utterly turn away from and renounce all their sins. I forgive all my ancestors for the effects of their sins on me and my children. I confess and renounce all of my own sins. I renounce and rebuke Satan and every spiritual power of his affecting me and my family.

I renounce and forsake all involvement in Freemasonry or any other lodge or craft by my ancestors and myself. I renounce witchcraft, the principal spirit behind Freemasonry, and I renounce Baphomet, the Spirit of Antichrist and the curse of the Luciferian doctrine. I renounce the idolatry, blasphemy, secrecy and deception of Masonry at every level. I specifically renounce the insecurity, the love of position and power, the love of money, avarice or greed, and the pride which would have led my ancestors into Masonry. I renounce all the fears which held them in Masonry, especially the fears of death, fears of men and fears of trusting, in the name of Jesus Christ.

I renounce every position held in the lodge by any of my ancestors, including "Tyler," "Master," "Worshipful Master," or any other. I renounce the calling of any man "Master," for Jesus Christ is my only master and Lord, and He forbids anyone else having that title. I renounce the entrapping of others into Masonry, and observing the helplessness of others during the rituals. I renounce the effects of Masonry passed on to me through any female ancestor who felt distrusted and rejected by her husband as he entered and attended any lodge and refused to tell her of his secret activities.

1st Degree

I renounce the oaths taken and the curses involved in the First or entered Apprentice degree, especially their effects on the throat and tongue. I renounce the Hoodwink, the blindfold, and its effects on emotions and eyes, including all confusion, fear of the dark, fear of the light, and fear of sudden noises. I renounce the secret word, BOAZ, and all it means. I renounce the mixing and mingling of truth and error, and the blasphemy of this degree of Masonry. I renounce the noose around the neck, the fear of choking and also every spirit causing asthma, hayfever, emphysema or any other breathing difficulty. I renounce the compass point, sword or spear held against the breast, the fear of death by stabbing pain, and the fear of heart attack from this degree.

In the name of Jesus Christ I now pray for healing of... (throat, vocal cords, nasal passages, sinus, bronchial tubes, etc.) for healing of the speech area, and the release of the Word of God to me and through me and my family.

2nd Degree

I renounce the oaths taken and the curses involved in the second or Fellow Craft degree of Masonry, especially the curses on the heart and chest. I renounce the secret words JACHIN and SHIBBOLETH and all that these mean. I cut off emotional hardness, apathy, indifference, unbelief, and deep anger from me and my family. In the name of Jesus Christ I pray for the healing of... (the chest/lung/heart area) and also for the healing of my emotions, and ask to be made sensitive to the Holy Spirit of God.

3rd Degree

I renounce the oaths taken and the curses involved in the third or Master Mason degree, especially the curses on the stomach and womb area. I renounce the secret words MAHA BONE, MACHABEN, MACHBINNA and TUBAL CAIN, and all that they mean. I renounce the Spirit of Death from the blows to the head enacted as ritual murder, the fear of death false martyrdom, fear of violent gang attack, assault, or rape, and the helplessness of this degree. I renounce the falling into the coffin or stretcher involved in the ritual of murder. I renounce the false resurrection of this degree, because only Jesus Christ is the Resurrection and the Life! I also renounce the blasphemous kissing of the Bible on a Witchcraft oath. I cut off all spirits of death, witchcraft and deception and in the name of Jesus Christ I pray for the healing of... (the stomach, gall bladder, womb, liver, and any other organs of my body affected by Masonry), and I ask for a release of compassion and understanding for me and my family.

Holy Royal Arch Degree

I renounce and forsake the oaths taken and the curses involved in the Holy Royal Arch Degree of Masonry, especially the oath regarding the removal of the head from the body and the exposing of the brains to the hot sun. I renounce the Mark Lodge, and the mark in the form of squares and angles which marks the person for life. I also reject the jewel or talisman which may have been made from this mark sign and worn at lodge meetings. I renounce the false secret name of God, JAHBULON, and the password, AMMIRUHAMAH and all they mean. I renounce the false communion or Eucharist taken in this degree, and all the mockery, skepticism and unbelief about the redemptive work of Jesus Christ on the cross of Calvary. I cut off all these curses and their effects on me and my family in the name of Jesus Christ, and I pray for... (healing of the brain, the mind, etc.)

18th Degree

I renounce the oaths taken and the curses involved in the eighteenth degree of Masonry, the Most Wise Sovereign Knight of the Pelican and the Eagle and Sovereign Prince Rose Croix of Heredom. I renounce and reject the Pelican witchcraft spirit as well as the occultic influence of the Rosicrucians and the Kabbala in this degree. I renounce the claim that the death of Jesus Christ was a "dire calamity," and also the deliberate mockery and twisting of the Christian doctrine of the Atonement. I renounce the blasphemy and rejection of the deity of Jesus Christ, and the secret words IGNE NATURA RENOVATUR INTEGRA and its burning. I renounce the mockery of the communion taken in this degree, including a biscuit, salt and white wine.

30th Degree

I renounce the oaths taken and the curses involved in the thirtieth degree of

Masonry the Grand Knight Kadosh and Knight of the Black and White Eagle. I renounce the password, "STIBIUM ALKABAR," and all it means.

31st Degree

I renounce the oaths taken and the curses involved in the thirty-first degree of Masonry, the Grand Inspector Inquisitor Commander. I renounce all the gods and goddesses of Egypt which are honored in this degree, including Anubis with the ram's head, Osiris the Sun god, Isis the sister and wife of Osiris and also the moon goddess. I renounce the Soul of Cheres, the false symbol of immortality, the Chamber of the dead and the false teaching of reincarnation.

32nd Degree

I renounce the oaths taken and the curses involved in the thirty-second degree of Masonry, the Sublime Prince of the Royal Secret. I renounce Masonry's false trinitarian deity AUM, and its parts; Brahma the creator, Vishnu the preserver and Shiva the destroyer. I renounce the deity of AHURA-MAZDA, the claimed spirit or source of all light, and the worship with fire, which is an abomination to God, and drinking from a human skull in some Rites.

York Rite

I renounce the oaths taken and the curses involved in the York Rite of

Freemasonry, including Mark Master, Past Master, Most Excellent Master, Royal Master, Select Master, Super Excellent Master, the Orders of the Red Cross, the Knights of Malta, and the Knights Templar degrees. I renounce the secret words of JOPPA, KEB RAIOTH, and MAHER-SHALAL-HASHBAZ. I renounce the vows taken on a human skull, the crossed swords, and the curse and death wish of Judas of having the head cut off and placed on top of a church spire. I renounce the unholy communion and especially of drinking from a human skull in some Rites.

Shriners (America only – doesn't apply in other countries).

I renounce the oaths taken and the curses and penalties involved in the Ancient Arabic Order of the Nobles of the Mystic Shrine. I renounce the piercing of the eyeballs with a three-edged blade, the flaying of the feet, the madness, and the worship of the false god Allah as the god of our fathers. I renounce the hoodwink, the mock hanging, the mock beheading, the mock drinking of the blood of the victim, the mock dog urinating on the initiate, and the offering of urine as a commemoration.

33rd Degree

I renounce the oaths taken and the curses involved in the thirty-third degree of

Masonry, the Grand Sovereign Inspector General. I renounce and forsake the declaration that Lucifer is God. I renounce the cable-tow around the neck. I renounce the death wish that the wine drunk from a human skull should turn to poison and the skeleton whose cold arms are invited if the oath of this degree is violated. I renounce the three infamous assassins of their grand master, law, property and religion, and the greed and witchcraft involved in the attempt to manipulate and control the rest of mankind..

All other degrees

I renounce all the other oaths taken, the rituals of every other degree and the curses involved. I renounce all other lodges and secret societies such as Prince Hall FreemasonryMormonism, The Order of Amaranth, Oddfellows, Buffalos, Druids, Foresters, Orange, Elks, Moose and Eagles Lodges, the Ku Klux Klan, The Grange, the Woodmen of the World, Rider of the Red Robe, the Knights of Pythias, the Mystic Order of the Veiled Prophets of the Enchanted Realm, the women's Orders of the Eastern Star, and of the White Shrine of Jerusalem, the girls' order of the Daughters of the Eastern Star, the International Orders of Job's Daughters, and of the Rainbow, and the boys' Order of De Molay, and their effects on me and all my family.

I renounce the ancient pagan teaching and symbolism of the First Tracing Board, the Second Tracing Board and the Third Tracing Board used in the ritual of the Blue Lodge. I renounce the pagan ritual of the "Point with a Circle" with all its bondages and phallus worship. I renounce the occultic mysticism of the black and white mosaic checkered floor with the tessellated pagan symbolism and bondages. I renounce and utterly forsake the Great Architect Of The Universe, who is revealed in the higher degrees as Lucifer, and his false claim to be the universal fatherhood of God. I also renounce the false claim that Lucifer is the Morning Star and Shining One and I declare that Jesus Christ is the Bright and Morning Star of Revelation 22:16.

I renounce the All-Seeing Third Eye of Freemasonry or Horus in the forehead and its pagan and occult symbolism. I renounce all false communions taken, all mockery of the redemptive work of Jesus Christ on the cross of Calvary, all unbelief, confusion and depression, and all worship of Lucifer as God. I renounce and forsake the lie of Freemasonry that man is not sinful, but just imperfect, and so can redeem himself through good works. I rejoice that the Bible states that I cannot do a single thing to earn my salvation, but that I can only be saved by grace through faith in Jesus Christ and what He accomplished on the Cross of Calvary.

I renounce all fear of insanity, anguish,

death wishes, suicide and death in the name of Jesus Christ. Death was conquered by Jesus Christ, and He alone holds the keys of death and hell, and I rejoice that He holds my life in His hands now He came to give me life abundantly and eternally, and I believe His promises.

I renounce all anger, hatred murderous thoughts, revenge, retaliation, spiritual apathy, false religion, all unbelief, especially unbelief in the Holy Bible as God's Word, and all compromise of God's Word. I renounce all spiritual searching into false religions, and all striving to please God. I rest in the knowledge that I have found my Lord and Savior Jesus Christ, and that He has found me.

I will burn all objects in my possession which connect me with all lodges and occultic organizations, including Masonry, Witchcraft and Mormonism, and all regalia, aprons, books of rituals, rings and other jewelry. I renounce the effects these or other objects of Masonry, such as the compass, the square, the noose or the blindfold, have had on me or my family, in Jesus Name.

(All participants should now be invited to sincerely carry out the following:
1) Symbolically remove the blindfold (hoodwink) and give it to the Lord for disposal;
2) in the same way, symbolically remove

the veil of mourning;
3) Symbolically cut and remove the noose from around the neck, gather it up with the cable-tow running down the body and give it all to the Lord for His disposal;
4) Renounce the false Freemasonry marriage covenant, removing from the 4th finger of the right hand the ring of this false marriage covenant, giving it to the Lord to dispose of it;
5) Symbolically remove the chains and bondages of Freemasonry from your body;
6) Symbolically remove all Freemasonry regalia and armor, especially the Apron;
7) Invite participants to repent of and seek forgiveness for having walked on all unholy ground, including Freemasonry lodges and temples, including any Mormon or other occultic/Masonic organization;
8) Symbolically remove the ball and chain from the ankles
9) Proclaim that Satan and his demons no longer have any legal rights to mislead and manipulate the person/s seeking help.)

Holy Spirit, I ask that you show me anything else which I need to do or to pray so that I and my family may be totally free from the consequences of the sins of Masonry, Witchcraft, Mormonism and Paganism.

(Pause, while listening to God, and pray as the Holy Spirit leads you)

Now dear Father God, I ask humbly for the blood of Jesus Christ, your Son, to cleanse me from all these sins I have confessed and renounced, to cleanse my spirit, my soul, my mind, my emotions, and every part of my body which has been affected by these sins, in Jesus' name!

I renounce every evil spirit association with Masonry and Witchcraft and all other sins, and I command in the name of Jesus Christ for Satan and every evil spirit to be bound and to leave me now, touching or harming no-one, and go to the place appointed for you by the Lord Jesus, never to return to me or my family. I call on the name of the Lord Jesus to be delivered of these spirits, in accordance with the many promises of the Bible. I ask to be delivered of every spirit of sickness, infirmity, curse, affliction, addiction, disease or allergy associated with theses sins I have confessed and renounced.

I surrender to God's Holy Spirit and to no other spirit all the places in my life where these sins have been. I ask you, Lord, to baptize me in your Holy Spirit now according to the promises in your Word. I take to myself the whole armor of God in accordance with Ephesians Chapter Six, and rejoice in its protection as Jesus surrounds me and fills me with His Holy Spirit. I enthrone you, Lord Jesus, in my heart, for you are my Lord and my Savior, the source of eternal life. Thank you, Father God, for your mercy, your forgiveness and your love, in the name of Jesus Christ, Amen."[15]

This book is in no wise meant to be an exhaustive study of Freemasonry. It is presented simply as a brief overview in order for the Christian to understand the forces he/she is dealing with. For more thorough examination of this subject I suggest the following materials:

The Dark Side Of Freemasonry, by Ed Decker (Huntington House)

The Secret Teachings of the Masonic Lodge – A Christian Perspective, by John Ankerberg and John Weldon (Moody Press)

Unmasking Freemasonry – Removing the Hoodwink, by Selwyn Stevens Jubilee)

Inside the Brotherhood, by Martin Short (Harper Collins)

The Deadly Deception, by Jim Shaw and Tom C. McKenney (Hungtington House)

Scarlet and the Beast. Volumes I, II, and III, by John Daniel (JKI Publishing)

Unmasking Freemasonry – Removing the Hoodwink, by Selwyn Stevens Jubilee)

Endnotes

1 Albert G. Mackey, Encyclopedia of Freemasonry (The Masonic History Company, 1921), p. 516.

2 Walvoord, John F., and Zuck, Roy B., The Bible Knowledge Commentary, (Wheaton, Illinois: Scripture Press Publications, Inc.) 1983, 1985.

3 Albert Pike was a 33rd Degree Mason, Grand Commander of the Accepted Scottish Rite of Freemasonry from 1859-1891. He wrote Morals and Dogma for the Supreme Council of the Thirty-Third as stated in its title pages. He was considered the foremost authority on the doctrine of the Scottish Rite of Freemasonry,

4 Albert Pike, Morals and Dogma (Richmond, L. H. Jenkins, Inc., 1924), p. 368.

5 Pike, p. 213.

6 George Thornburgh, et al., Masonic Monitor, 7th edition (Arkansas, Democrat P. & L. Co. Little Rock, 1919), p. 21.

7 Thornburgh, p. 25.

8 Thornburgh, pp. 21-22.

9 Pike, p. 333.

10 Pike, p. 819.

11 “Do Freemasons Worship Satan?” Instructions to the 23 Supreme Councils of the World, July 15, 1889. (Recorded by A. C. De La Rive in La Femme et l’Enfant dans la FrancMaconnerie Universelle on page 588): 3, online, Internet, 23 November 1997.

12 Pike, p. 321

13 The Proceedings of the United States Anti-Masonic Convention: held in Philadelphia, September 11, 1830 (Montague, Massachusetts, Acacia Press, Inc. 1996). 16, online, internet, 20 November 1987.

APPENDIX

Testimony of **Marlin Foura** **8/10/98**

My involvement with Freemasonry started nearly two decades ago when my older brother shared with me his involvement in this organization. At that time in my life I was self-employed and struggling to make ends meet. It was explained to me that there was an organization of men that upheld and supported each other through this thing called the Blue Lodge of Freemasonry. Well, the promise or at least the opportunity for my business to turn around lured me into this organization where I was told all kinds of successful business people from our region were united and met once per month. Greed took hold deeply.

Although both my brother and myself were raised in a Christian home with God-fearing parents, I never asked their opinion. I felt I had to make it on my own never seeking advice from them or God. I went through the required steps and was raised in the Blue Lodge as a master mason. From there I went through the required steps of the Scottish Rite and attained a 32nd degree.

Years went by quickly and I realized that I had made some friends, met some successful people, met some not so successful people, and started to ask some questions:

a. Why are we not to talk about religion, God, or church in the Blue Lodge?
b. Why is there racial prejudice in the Lodge?
c. Why is there a sense that if you're not a mason, you're a second-class person?

This stuff did not line up with the way I was brought up. I frequented the lodge less and less, until stopping completely any attendance to a meeting or function sponsored by a Masonic organization.

Then one day I heard Randy Clark was ministering in the Harrisburg, PA. area and felt a strong need to attend. During the altar call a comment he made was, *"...that people involved in Freemasonry needed to come forth for prayer to break the strongholds the enemy has through that organization."* Well, I went forward – but not for deliverance – but to get a closer look at this guy. Something inside of me stirred and said, *"he's wrong – Freemasonry is based on Christian Principles – Don't listen to him!"* I left that night feeling confused, asking myself, *"why did he say that?"* I figured I would pray about that and visit his meetings in State College, PA., three or four weeks later.

During the meetings in State College, Randy again mentioned the things about masons. This time I felt sick on the inside. Something was in there and stirring. I left the meetings that first night and looked at this book, *Unto Death*[2], but did not purchase it. I made myself a promise that I would return tomorrow, and if they still had one left, I would purchase it. I purchased it the following day.

On Tuesday during my lunch hour at work, I decided to read it. I started to read "Unto Death" with a very critical spirit towards what it would say, and I began to mark up the book with flags (red ink) in areas that I thought were derogatory toward masons. On or about the second flag, the Holy Spirit spoke to me, and I felt a very strong desire to read on objectively. Within twenty minutes I was very sick to my stomach to point of throwing up. Through my tears and weeping aloud I came to the realization that I had done many things against God in the oaths of Freemasonry, and started crying out, *"Oh God forgive me!"*

The thing I felt stirring earlier within my body cavity revealed themselves – demons – clawing at my stomach and intestinal area like cats claws tearing at me for several minutes. Instantly, I realized that I was being physically attacked by demons and cried out to God for help. It felt as if a dagger was thrust into my lower right stomach cavity, and then twisted. I instantly felt the urgent need to run to the rest room to throw up and to relieve myself. I moved very quickly to that area and upon arriving there I realized that I was bleeding profusely. I cried out again to the Lord for help. I began to rebuke the evil spirits which were attacking me, in the name of Jesus. I don't remember how many times I did that, but the tearing at my insides finally subsided.

As I sat there, and eventually stood up, I just stared at the blood all over the toilet, and wishing that I was in my pastor's office which would be a safe place to finish breaking off any remaining demons. After cleaning myself up, and cleaning up the rest room area, I immediately telephoned the associate pastor of our church, and told him what had happened. I also told him that I was being physically attacked by demons and was in need of immediate prayer and intercession. We scheduled an appointment for the following day, Wednesday at 10:00 A.M., and I requested that both he and the senior pastor be there. Before this scheduled meeting took place, the Holy Spirit revealed to the associate pastor the situation at hand. He actually purchased a copy of the book, "Unto Death", the same night I had called him.

Immediately after making this phone call, fear began to creep in, and I was afraid to go anywhere except to church. I asked my wife to read the book when she got home from the office. She was shocked. I told her about the demonic attack that had taken place, and about my fear of sleep that night. My wife held me and prayed for me throughout the night. After several hours, maybe around 2 or 3 a.m., I felt the fear beginning to lift, and was able to get a few hours rest.

Unto Death

Wednesday morning found me tired, weak, and trembling, and praying for 10 a.m. to arrive – soon! I arrived at the church on time, clutching the "Unto Death" book, and wanting nothing but total deliverance. After a brief time of sharing, our senior pastor skimmed through the book. Horror gripped his features, and the realization of the need for deliverance prayer became very apparent. The three of us, the pastor, associate pastor, and myself spent the next few hours in prayer and celebration worship, as I renounced all involvement in Freemasonry, past positions held, oaths taken, and witchcraft of this organization. During the time spent on the floor, on my face before God, and the prayers being spoken over me, I received a fresh revelation of God's love for me.

I realized that for all those years spent in opposition to God, He was there all the time watching out for me, loving me, and longing for a relationship with me. I know that God revealed His love to me that day – forgave me of my sin and SET ME FREE!

I will always worship the Lord God Jehovah-Shalom – my peace, and Jehovah-Rophe –my healer, and as Jehovah-Rohi – my shepherd, and will praise His Son for His redeeming work on the cross. Believing on Christ Jesus is the only way to be totally free.

In God's love,
Your new brother in Christ,
Marlin L. Foura

***Testimony of* Jean Aardahl 4/1/99**

The words, "It's not true; it's not true!" were the words I cried out from my heart when I found out the Mormon temple ceremonies were birthed from Freemasonry. During my years as a Mormon I was told that there was not any connection between Mormonism and Freemasonry. Yet I knew Joseph Smith, Hyrum Smith, Brigham Young and many other Mormon leaders in early foundational Mormonism has been Masons at one time.

My husband and I were not born into Mormonism but had a Christian background in our youth. We found Mormonism while searching for a church to attend like a lot of young people. The family values and good wholesome living style appealed to us [and] also the Lord was talked about a lot. Little did we know or understand the true foundations of Mormonism, just enough of truth to entice and blind.

I had left the large downtown Sacramento library when I cried out to the Lord with the new found information I had read in the reference section under 'secret societies.' There were numerous books with large numbers of secret societies and their practices. I was totally unprepared for what I had found out about the Masonic lodge rites and the Mormon temple ceremonies being so much alike.

This was the final thing God used to open my blind eyes concerning Mormonism. It was [as] if blinders came off my eyes and mind and I could see and think clearly. I had a choice now and I could no longer deny Mormonism was not of the real and true living God. The Lord knew I would need something so concrete to take the next step, which was to admit Mormonism was not true and to leave it, knowing the heavy price I was to pay—my husband and family.

When I told my husband about my concerns, he told me he would divorce me. Now that I absolutely knew Mormonism was not true, I knew what it meant. The Lord spoke to me in the middle of my crisis when my husband did try to divorce me and said, "There will be no divorce!" Through two divorce attempts and several hard years, the Lord was faithful.

My husband worked for the Mormon Church when all this was taking place with me. His anger turned into depression; eventually he came out of Mormonism but was disillusioned and wanted nothing to do with 'God' for a long time. As time went by he was watching me and starting to think maybe there was a truth to what I had been telling him about the Lord Jesus.

In November 1997, he became born again at a crusade we had attended and baptized at our home church. As time passed by, he was not free—his thinking was not clear and he did not have any desire to read the Bible or pray. Several months had passed and he was not free.

A guest speaker came to our church and brought a book on Freemasonry[3]. I bought it because of our Mormon background little knowing how it would impact our lives. I quickly read it that Sunday afternoon, knowing immediately my husband needed to read what I had found. As soon as he read the book, we knew we both needed to read and renounce Freemasonry together. My husband experienced immediate freedom in his mind to think clearly about the real gospel of Jesus Christ. My experience was minor compared to his. I noticed a big change in him with prayer, reading The Word and freedom to talk about Jesus and the Gospel.

We were led by a series of events to take a careful, long look at the Mormon temple ceremonies and were surprised at what we found. I had always known of the Masonic connection since leaving Mormonism but even I was surprised at the bondages that went beyond Freemasonry.

Appendix

By reading Barbara Cassada's book, Unto Death. I felt a need for my husband and myself to renounce Mormonism but way beyond what I had originally thought. We again sat down one Sunday afternoon and renounced what it required for a person to believe in Mormonism and next we renounced the Mormon temple ceremonies. The results was astounding. The biggest change I noticed in my husband was his immediate willingness to commit to Jesus as Savior and Lord of his life. He wanted to attend church and fellowship with other Christians. He wanted to participate in Church activities and talk about the Gospel and Jesus Christ openly and without being defensive. He was happy and free. I was helped with yielding to submission to a Church and authority. Until this renunciation I was always reserved and held back not knowing what was the problem. Now we were free!!!

---

[1] Testimony of Marlin Foura Ó1998 Barbara Cassada

[2] Barbara Cassada, *Unto Death: Freemasonry…Freedom in Christ or Bondage to Lucifer?,* published by the author, 1998

[3] Cassada

CPSIA information can be obtained
at www.ICGtesting.com
Printed in the USA
BVOW09s2313271217
503692BV00001B/78/P